James Monroe

A Captivating Guide to the Founding Father Who Served as the Fifth President of the United States

Free Bonus from Captivating History (Available for a Limited time)

Hi History Lovers!

Now you have a chance to join our exclusive history list so you can get your first history ebook for free as well as discounts and a potential to get more history books for free! Simply visit the link below to join.

Captivatinghistory.com/ebook

Also, make sure to follow us on:

Twitter: @Captivhistory

Facebook: Captivating History:@captivatinghistory

Contents

Introduction

From plantation owner to diplomat to U.S. President, James Monroe was known for his tenacity in pursuing what he thought was right, while also being honored for his fair policies, such as the Monroe Doctrine and policies to develop the country's infrastructure. These traits were recognized in 1816, when the West African country of Liberia, changed its name to Monrovia, in honor of James Monroe. It serves as the only international capital named after a U.S. President, and only one of two capitals in the world named after a U.S. President—the other being Washington, D.C.

James Monroe shares another badge of honor with George Washington in that the two were both unchallenged candidates for the presidency. Washington ran unopposed for his second presidential term in 1792 and Monroe held the same honor in 1820.

In losing both parents during his teenage years, Monroe was forced to drop out of school to help with his younger siblings. Despite this, he later attended college and went to law school. That he was counted on for his diplomatic skills demonstrates his sense of fairness, and paved the way for his presidency.

The United States, in its infancy during his lifetime, gained its foothold in history thanks to people like James Monroe and the peers of his day: George Washington, Patrick Henry, Thomas Jefferson, John Quincy Adams and James Madison.

James Monroe is probably best known for the Monroe Doctrine, a policy challenging European colonization and interference, but he was also an integral part of many other policies such as the Missouri Compromise.

Regardless of where his focus was required, Monroe met challenges head-on, whether it was working to improve the infrastructure of the country during his presidency, or working to end unjust practices such as the British impressment of U.S. sailors.

A family man, a diplomat, a soldier, a lawyer, a farmer and a president... no matter what capacity he was called on to serve, James Monroe did so with confidence and tireless perseverance.

Chapter 1 – His Early Years

James Monroe was born on April 28, 1758, during the fervor to colonize North America. His birthplace, in Westmoreland County, Virginia, was a partially wooded area of the colony.

Long before his birth, his family moved to Virginia to live in the 'virtual paradise,' as described in one 1649 pamphlet that circulated in London. Monroe's paternal grandfather emigrated from Scotland and began working a large piece of land in the area, while his maternal grandfather emigrated to Virginia from Wales.

By the time Monroe was born to Spence Monroe and Elizabeth Jones, the family owned 600 acres of land that Spence was farming. By many standards, the Monroe family would be considered upper-class, due to the fact that Spence owned land and slaves. Monroe also had four siblings: Elizabeth, Spence, Andrew and Joseph.

His mother taught Monroe and his siblings—Elizabeth, Spence, Andrew and Joseph—during their early years and when Monroe was 11, he was allowed to enroll in Campbelltown Academy, a school run by Reverend Archibald Campbell. Monroe was known as a bright pupil, excelling in Latin and mathematics.

Even then, he was drawn to friends who would later be politically inclined, including classmate John Marshall, who became the fourth Chief Justice of the United States, serving in that position from 1801 to 1835.

Despite his love of learning and his close friendships, Monroe was only involved with the school for parts of the year, since he was often needed at home to work on the farm. When he was 16, he left the school permanently, being thrust into adulthood following his mother's death, soon followed by his father's death.

Monroe inherited his family's farm and at least one slave, but he was still too young to manage such responsibilities.

His sister, Elizabeth, had already married, and Joseph Jones, their mother's brother, took in the three Monroe boys. Childless himself, Joseph not only acted like a surrogate parent, but also had a major influence on the direction that Monroe's life took. A member of the House of Burgesses himself, Joseph introduced James to influential Virginians, including George Washington, Patrick Henry and Thomas Jefferson.

Joseph also enrolled Monroe in the College of William and Mary in 1774. Perhaps ironically, the college would later grasp on to a bit of his history by purchasing the plantation he owned in later life.

If he had expected a peaceful college tenure, Monroe would have been wrong. By 1774, unrest had seized the hearts of the colonists. Britain enacted a series of restrictive laws after the Boston Tea Party. The "Intolerable Acts" as they became known, took away the self-governance of Massachusetts colonists, but incited fury throughout the 13 colonies.

Monroe himself became involved in the opposition to Lord John Murray, the 4th Earl of Dunmore, who was serving as the governor of Virginia at the time. Perhaps in anticipation of an uprising, Lord Dunmore ordered the removal of military supplies from the Hanover militia.

The act backfired, and Lord Dunmore took his family and fled the Governor's Palace, which was then raided by Monroe and other college classmates. They seized swords and an estimated 200 muskets for the militia.

Two years later, in 1776, Monroe dropped out of college and joined the Continental Army in the 3rd Virginia Regiment. Although he hadn't finished college, his intelligence and aptitude earned him the rank of lieutenant, serving under Captain George Washington.

He would later study law, but would never return to the college classroom. However, at 18 years old, Monroe was well on his way to making his mark on American history.

Chapter 2 – The Revolutionary War

As a lieutenant, Monroe had several months of training before his regiment was called north where they participated in two battles, known as the New York and New Jersey Campaign.

In the fight for control over New York City and New Jersey, Washington's troops were pushed back over the Potomac River by the British, under the command of General Sir William Howe.

Although morale was low and the winter was brutal on the soldiers, the Continental army regrouped and went on the attack again, this time on a Hessian encampment. Although they were stealthy, Monroe and Washington's cousin, William Washington, caught the attention of a local farmer and doctor John Riker. Learning that they were American soldiers on their way to a surprise attack, Dr. Riker joined them, assuming that he might be of some use.

The attack was successful but James was shot in the shoulder. An artery was severed and he was bleeding profusely. Fortunately, the doctor that they encountered on their way to the attack was on hand and stopped the bleeding, essentially saving Monroe's life.

The battle was deemed a victory for the patriots, and an estimated 900 Hessians were killed. However, there were many casualties on the American side as well, which were depicted in the famous painting *The Capture of the Hessians at Trenton, December 26, 1776*, by John Trumbull. In the painting, Monroe is captured as being attended to by Dr. Riker.

He was also depicted in another famous painting called *Washington Crossing the Delaware* by Emanuel Gottlieb Leutze. In it, Monroe is credited as the man who was holding the flag. However, some historians insist that Monroe crossed the Delaware well beyond Washington's famed crossing.

For his efforts, Monroe was promoted to the rank of captain and sent home to recover from his injuries. Under his new role, he also began to recruit soldiers for his own company, but was unsuccessful.

To that end, he asked to be returned to the front and started working with General William Alexander, also known as Lord Stirling. During this time, he also befriended the Marquis de Lafayette, a young Frenchman who volunteered his efforts against the British in retaliation for the killing of his father in the Seven Years War.

Lafayette induced Monroe to view war as the resistance to political tyranny, which no doubt influenced Monroe's actions in the political arena. The two remained close, and their friendship would prove fortuitous later during the French Revolution.

Monroe returned to battle and fought in the Philadelphia Campaign, an effort to capture the city, which was, at the time, where the Second Continental Congress was located. On the British side, the British General William Howe succeeded in the campaign, although his slow progress was heavily criticized for not coming to the aid of John Burgoyne's troops in a campaign that essentially forced the French to join the war.

During that campaign, Monroe met up with his old school chum, John Marshall, and the two hunkered down to wait out the brutal winter in the same quarters at the Valley Forge encampment.

In the summer of 1778, Monroe participated in the Battle of Monmouth. Perhaps ironically after surviving the brutal winter, the New Jersey battle ushered in soaring temperatures and killed many soldiers on both sides.

Constantly facing financial challenges, Monroe decided to resign his commission later that year. He wasn't out of action for long, though, because in December 1778, the British captured Savannah and his home state took steps to raise four regiments.

Bolstered with letters of recommendation from former commanders Washington and Stirling, as well as a letter from Alexander Hamilton, James returned to Virginia to try to get his own command. Although he was made lieutenant-colonel of one of the regiments, he faced the same struggle as he did after his injury at Trenton: he couldn't recruit enough men to join his regiment.

Once again, his challenges turned into an opportunity. His uncle suggested that he change career directions and start studying law, which would later bolster his political ambitions. Monroe moved to Williamsburg and by 1780, was studying law under Thomas Jefferson, who was then the governor of Virginia.

Monroe never entirely relished the idea of practicing law, but he was very interested in politics, and was convinced that establishing a law practice was the most practical way to advance his political career.

While studying with Jefferson, Monroe accompanied him to Richmond, where the state capital was now established, largely because it would be easier to defend from the British, who were starting to concentrate their focus on the southern colonies.

The governor named Monroe a colonel in the army and he was expected, once again, to recruit men. For the third time, he was unsuccessful. Monroe returned home, and wasn't present when the British raided Richmond in 1781.

Then, the war turned a corner. It was at the Siege of Yorktown where Lafayette held Cornwallis' troops with his own army of 5,000 American soldiers, with an additional 1,500 French troops. With Washington's forces 200 miles away, Lafayette was ordered to prevent the British forces from escaping. They did so until Washington could arrive in early September, surrounding the British army.

To Monroe's frustration, he also missed the Siege of Yorktown, which proved to be the final battle of the Revolutionary War.

By this point, though, Monroe's tenure with the war was over and he moved on to a new phase in his life.

Chapter 3 – Early Political Career and Family Life

James Monroe passed the Virginia bar exam and began practicing law in Fredericksburg, an effort partially funded by the sale of the plantation he had inherited.

At the same time, he won his first political appointment and in 1782, was elected to the Virginia House of Delegates, the successor to the House of Burgesses, of which his uncle was a member.

He first served on the state's Executive Council and the following year, was elected to the Congress of the Confederation, the governing party of the United States, where he served until his tenure concluded three years later.

While serving in Congress, he became interested in the country's expansion west and was part of the governing body that wrote the legislation for the Northwest Ordinance, the first organized area of the United States.

In 1776, he married Elizabeth Kortright, the daughter of Lawrence and Hannah Kortright. The family was wealthy, although they had taken a hit financially because Lawrence was considered by many to have loyalist sympathies.

Her father's political views hardly affected James when he met the beautiful Elizabeth at a local theatre. When they married, Elizabeth was 17, nine years younger than James.

The two were married in her father's home in a ceremony presided over by Reverend Benjamin Moore, the second Episcopal bishop of New York. Interestingly, while his participation with the Monroe marriage was noteworthy, Reverend Moore is best remembered for giving communion to Alexander Hamilton on his deathbed, after Hamilton was mortally wounded in a duel with Aaron Burr, then the Vice President of the United States.

James and Elizabeth honeymooned on Long Island and then returned to New York City where they lived with her father until Congress adjourned that year.

It was perhaps a bittersweet time for Elizabeth's father, Lawrence, who never remarried after losing his wife, Hannah in childbirth. Elizabeth had four older siblings. No doubt the house felt empty when James resigned from Congress with the intent to return to his legal career in Virginia.

Lawrence was in New York with Elizabeth gave birth to their first child, Eliza Kortright Monroe, in December 1776. James Spence Monroe was born two years later, but died when he was 16 months old. Historians did not record the cause of death, but it is known that he was sick for several days before he succumbed to his illness.

"An unhappy event has occurr'd which has overwhelmed us with grief," James Monroe wrote to his friend, James Madison in 1800. "At ten last night our beloved babe departed this life after several days sickness… I cannot give you an idea of the effect this event has produc'd on my family, or of my own affliction… This has roused me beyond what I thought was possible… [sic]"

Despite the devastation, time continued on. James and Elizabeth had another daughter in 1804, whom they named Marie Hester Monroe. Although they could not have known it at the time, Marie would later be the first presidential child to be married in the White House.

After moving back to Virginia, Monroe became a state attorney, and then chose to serve another term in the Virginia House of Delegates.

In 1788, Monroe was selected as a delegate to the Virginia Ratifying Convention, a group of 168 members who met to determine if they would ratify or vote against the proposed United States Constitution. After deliberating from June 2 through June 27, the Virginia convention narrowly voted to ratify the convention, making it the tenth state to ratify the Constitution.

Monroe was one of the 79 members to cast his vote against ratification, largely because he supported the addition of a bill of rights, which was not included at that time. Monroe, like others, feared that a central government could cast a shadow over the rights of individual states.

James and the other anti-federalists (although they called themselves "federalists for amendments") weren't ready to give up the fight and planned to put in power a Congress that would amend the newly-adopted Constitution. Under the urging of Patrick Henry who vehemently opposed ratification, James ran against James Madison for a seat in the First United States Congress.

Although they were political opponents, the two maintained their friendship and often traveled together. When the vote was held, Madison was elected by more than 300 votes.

Monroe decided that it was time for another change.

After the defeat, Monroe returned to his law practice and also took up farming in Charlottesville, but not for long. In 1790, Senator William Grayson died. Only one of two elected senators who voted against ratifying the Constitution, perhaps it was only natural for Monroe to be elected to finish out Grayson's term.

After the term was completed, Monroe went on to win the reelection in 1791, a position he held until he was asked to bring his diplomatic talents overseas.

Chapter 4 – Ambassador to France

War was once again on the horizon, but not on the young United States' shores. In the late 1790s, the French Revolutionary Wars loomed, and conflicts with both Britain and France were impacting trade with the United States.

In response to these foreign concerns, Washington, who was serving as president, appointed two new ambassadors in 1794. Federalist John Jay was named the ambassador to the United Kingdom and James Monroe was sent to France as the United States ambassador in that country.

Not one to be separated from his family for extended periods, Monroe gathered his family and traveled to France. Prior to their departure, Elizabeth gave herself a crash course in French culture to make sure that she did not offend society. She need not have worried—between her diligent studies and her American charm; she was given the nickname "La Belle Américaine."

Elizabeth's love for the French was evidenced in later years as she adopted many European customs when serving as First Lady. For example, each guest who dined with them had their own servant, as was the norm in French aristocracy, and the family frequently conversed in French.

It was a precarious time in France, to be sure, but Monroe was confident enough in his diplomatic skills to not only keep his family safe, but to also assist others who had become victims of the French Revolution.

Thomas Paine was instrumental in influencing people in the colonies to revolt against the British with his popular pamphlet, *Common Sense*. His nature to incite rebellion followed him to Britain after the American Revolution and then to France, where he was elected to the French National Convention, supposedly without being able to speak French.

Paine's fervent writings got him in hot water once more, this time in France. In 1791, he released *Rights of Man,* highlighting his perspective on the French Revolution. As he continued to condemn the revolutionaries who were executing hundreds via the guillotine, the government that once supported him turned against him.

In December 1793, Paine was arrested and imprisoned in Luxembourg Prison, a move that caught the attention of Ambassador Monroe.

Upon Monroe's arrival in France, one of his first tasks was addressing the French National Convention, giving a speech on the benefits of republicanism. He received a standing ovation for his efforts and used this and other successes to secure Paine's release from prison.

Not one to sit still herself, Elizabeth Monroe took it upon herself to visit Adrienne de Lafayette, the wife of Monroe's good friend from the American Revolution.

Madame Lafayette was also imprisoned in 1792, following a movement to control all nobles. At first, she was placed under house arrest, but after the 1794 Reign of Terror, she was transferred to La Force Prison. She was comparatively fortunate: her grandmother, mother and sister were all executed. However, diplomacy prevailed in her situation and after several months at La Force Prison, the Monroes were instrumental in her quiet release from prison.

The Lafayette family had already been granted American citizenship and upon her release, she and her family were given American passports.

While Monroe's time as ambassador saw many successes, including trade protection, it was a short-lived tenure. His counterpart in Britain helped orchestrate the Jay Treaty between the U.S. and Britain. The ambassador to France was outraged because he was not fully informed of the treaty's nature, which damaged U.S. relations with France.

However, the Jay Treaty was quite beneficial for the United States, due to the many concessions the British made, including an agreement to leave the Northwest Territory. It also facilitated U.S. trade in the British East Indies and not only improved trade between Britain but also led it to agree to compensation for its acts against American shipping.

In return, the U.S. agreed that it would not fund privateers in ports hostile to British interests. The treaty also ordered those Americans who owed money to British merchants before the war to pay up.

Overall, the treaty was considered an important step to prevent future animosity between the two countries; however, those benefits did not console either Monroe or France. Washington called on James to convince the French that the treaty was benign, but the country was not convinced.

Frustrated, Washington demanded that Monroe return to the U.S., convinced that the ambassador was failing to "safeguard the interests of his country."

In return, Monroe harbored a concern that Washington's sensibility may have been compromised by his age.

Chapter 5 – James Monroe: Slave Owner

He and his family made the return voyage in November 1796, but being on home soil did not alleviate Monroe's frustration. He started to pen his experiences as ambassador, which turned into a 400-page defense. In it, he highlighted his concerns that the treaty, while strengthening ties with Britain, would undermine relations with France.

The family was also struggling financially. Although he received a stipend of $9,000 for living and working in France, they soon found that this wasn't enough to sustain them, between the higher cost of living and their social obligations. After all, the reason they were in the country was to maintain or even improve relations with the European country, so they could hardly cut corners and eliminate social engagements.

Just for the cost of passage home and to ship their belongings, Monroe was forced to take out a mortgage on his new home in Virginia.

For a while after his return, James concentrated his efforts on practicing law and farming. Prior to leaving for France, he purchased a 3,500-acre plantation in Albemarle abutting Jefferson's plantation. Although he had aspirations to build a mansion on the land, he ended up building a much more modest six-room house after his return to the U.S. It was supposed to be a temporary structure, but because he was on the move so much, his family ended up living in it for two decades.

The Ash Lawn-Highland is now simply known as Highland. While he often owned an estimated 30 to 40 slaves at any time, a common practice with large landowners in the south during that era, by 1810, he owned 49 slaves living at Highland. (At the time, his neighbor, Jefferson, owned 147 slaves.)

Because he was so often away from Highland due to his political duties, the plantation was frequently controlled by overseers and slaves were often swapped back and forth between Highland and another piece of property that Monroe owned.

In July 1826, *The Central Gazette* featured an advertisement for the capture and reward of two of Monroe's slaves. Known only as George and Phebe, the two escaped and were assumed to be making their way toward Loudon or heading toward a free state. "If taken in the county," the ad read, "I will give a reward of Ten Dollars: or Fifteen Dollars if taken out of the county and secured in any jail so that I get them again."

The two were never found.

Interestingly, Monroe's perspective on slavery was divided. While he depended on slaves and in his lifetime owned as many as 250 slaves, he never freed any of them. However, in a letter to John Mason in 1829, Monroe called slavery "one of the evils still remaining, incident to our Colonial system."

During Monroe's first year as president, the Society for the Colonization of Free People of Color of America—more commonly known as the American Colonization Society (ACS)—was created upon the premise of relocating freed slaves or free-born blacks to Africa. The colony was located on the Pepper Coast of West Africa.

Some felt that this was a veiled attempt at upholding slavery, but the organizers, which were mostly Quakers, felt that this provided the relocated colonists a better opportunity for freedom in Africa.

In just over the first two decades, 4,571 emigrants were sent across the ocean. Unfortunately, disease ran rampant and of those, there were less than 2,000 survivors by 1843. However, the colony did thrive and reached economic stability. In 1847, the area known by then as Liberia, declared its independence.

Because of his support of the ACS, the capital of Christopolis was renamed Monrovia and the name remains.

Many years later, Monroe was forced to sell Highlands in 1828. All of his slaves were also sold and sent further south, although it is unknown if the man who purchased them, Colonial Joseph White, honored Monroe's stipulation to keep the slave families together.

Chapter 6 – The Governorship & Return to France

In 1799, Monroe was elected to serve as the governor of Virginia. While the governor had fewer duties at this time, he was able to persuade the state to make some infrastructure improvements, such as making changes to transportation. He also urged the legislature to improve the educational system.

One of his primary duties was overseeing the militia when it was activated, but recalling the struggles the fledgling militia had in the beginning of the Revolutionary War, Monroe called for better training for the soldiers.

A year into office, he did call out the militia in response to what is now known as Gabriel's Rebellion, an effort by the slaves on a nearby plantation to rise against the slave owners. The rebellion was squashed and the slave Gabriel was hanged, along with 27 other slave conspirators.

In his letter to Jefferson on September 15, 1800, Monroe seemed to question the punishment. "We have had much trouble with the negroes here," he wrote. "The plan of an insurrection has been clearly proved, & appears to have been of considerable extent. Ten have been condemned & executed, and there are at least twenty perhaps forty more to be tried, of whose guilt no doubt is entertained. It is unquestionably the most serious and formidable conspiracy we have ever known of the kind: tho' indeed to call it so is to give no idea of the thing itself. While it was possible to keep it secret, wh[ich] it was till we saw the extent of it, we did so. But when it became indispensably necessary to resort to strong measures with a view to protect the town [Richmond], the publick arms, the Treasury and the Jail, wh[ich] were all threatened, the opposit course was in part tak[en]. We then made a display of our force and measures of defence with a view to intimidate those people. Where to arrest the hand of the Executioner, is a question of great importance. It is hardly to be presumed, a rebel who avows it was his intention to assassinate his master… if pardoned will ever become a useful servant and we have no power to transport him abroad—Nor is it less difficult to say whether mercy or severity is the better policy in this case, tho' where there is cause for doubt it is best to incline to the former council. I shall be happy to have y[our] opinion on these points [*sic*]."

In his response five days later, Jefferson mulled over Monroe's concerns. "Where to stay the hand of the executioner is an important question," he said. "Those who have escaped from the immediate danger, must have feelings which would dispose them to extend the executions. Even here, where every thing has been perfectly tranquil, but where a familiarity with slavery, and a possibility of danger from that quarter prepare the general mind for some severities, there is a strong sentiment that there has been hanging enough. The other states & the world at large will for ever condemn us if we indulge a principle of revenge, or go one step beyond absolute necessity. They cannot lose sight of the rights of the two parties, & the object of the unsuccessful one. Our situation is indeed a difficult one: for I doubt whether these people can ever be permitted to go at large among us with safety. To reprieve them and keep them in prison till the meeting of the legislature will encourage efforts for their release. Is there no fort & garrison of the state or of the Union, where they could be confined, & where the presence of the garrison would preclude all ideas of attempting a rescue. Surely the legislature would pass a law for their exportation, the proper measure on this &

all similar occasions? I hazard these thoughts for your own consideration only, as I should be unwilling to be quoted in the case; you will doubtless hear the sentiments of other persons & places, and will hence be enabled to form a better judgment on the whole than any of us singly & in a solitary situation."

Regardless of Monroe's concerns, the country felt it needed to do something to avoid further insurrections after Gabriel's Rebellion and even more restrictions were placed on blacks, whether slave or free. For example, they were forbidden to gather in groups, they could not be educated and they were forbidden from outside work.

Whether it was a disturbance with slaves or others, Monroe tried to balance what was fair and right. As Jefferson said, "Monroe was so honest that if you turned his soul inside out, there would not be a spot on it. [*sic*]"

While Gabriel's Rebellion was one of the notable points of Monroe's tenure as governor, he also made several other changes in this role. For example, he furthered an effort to create the state's first penitentiary, providing an alternative for even harsher punishments.

He also worked to enhance communication with the legislature by giving the first State of the Commonwealth address, once again setting a precedent for others to follow

A year into his governorship in 1780, Monroe threw his efforts into helping Thomas Jefferson win his bid for the presidency. Not only did he use his position to influence the state's presidential electors but he also toyed with the idea of using the militia to force a favorable outcome for Jefferson. The militia was not called out in the end, but it exemplifies how passionate Monroe could be when he took up a cause.

For his efforts, when Jefferson was elected president, he named Monroe as his Secretary of State.

Monroe's term wrapped up as governor and Jefferson reached out to him once again. This time, he asked Monroe to make "a temporary sacrifice to prevent the greatest of all evils in the present prosperous tide of our affairs." Jefferson sent James back to France to assist with the negotiations with France for the purchase of New Orleans. In 1800, France was given the Louisiana territory from Spain as part of the Treaty of San Ildefonso.

Since the city was so close to the mouth of the Mississippi River, the United States was determined to purchase New Orleans. And it was good timing, too. Napoleon Bonaparte would have loved to keep hold of it, but the country was still reeling from the high costs of war.

After much negotiation overseas, James was integral in the Louisiana Purchase, obtaining not just New Orleans but the entire territory of Louisiana—all 530 million acres of it— for the bargain price of $15 million.

Even though the U.S. government had initially authorized 50 million francs, just over $9 million at the time, the purchase was considered a huge win for America. Not only was New Orleans secured, but now the country had bragging rights to so much additional land, it was difficult at best to comprehend the parcel of land it just acquired—one that nearly doubled the size of the United States.

One of Monroe's main objectives during the four years he was a diplomat in Britain was to try to extend the Jay Treaty, the very treaty that he had so opposed when it was created.

By this time, the terms of the treaty had expired but by 1806, Monroe had effectively negotiated a new treaty with Britain. He was surprised to find that, after all that work, Jefferson refused to move it further for ratification. Although he was essentially told that he could do better in his negotiations, particularly since there was no clause to address U.S. seaman impressment, Monroe vehemently claimed that this was the best they could do with Britain.

It was a frustrating time for Monroe. Not only was he aggravated by Jefferson's rejection of his hard work in securing the best terms he could, but the news that his friend and neighbor was refusing to support the work he did to negotiate the new treaty was almost too much.

This also happened in addition to several challenging months when he traveled to Spain to try to convince the country that the Louisiana Purchase indeed included the western section of the Florida territory as well—a premise the Spaniards refused to consider.

So, when Monroe's tenure as the British ambassador was up, he returned home, prickling with frustration.

However, as luck would perhaps have it, 1808 was another presidential election year and Monroe was temporarily buoyed by the Old Republicans (also referred to as Quids) to run against his friend, James Madison, for the Democratic-Republican nomination.

Some say that Monroe's campaign was in a halfhearted retaliation for what he felt was Madison's lack of support for his failed treaty attempt. Other historians champion Monroe for stating their similarities, with the exception to foreign policy issues.

Regardless, Madison won his party's nomination and became the fourth president of the United States. Monroe, ever moving forward, was elected to the Virginia House of Delegates in 1810 and then served as Governor of Virginia for most of 1811 when he was once again called on by a president – this time, Madison sought his help.

If one assumed that there was any animosity between the two, it was quickly squelched when, three years into his tenure as president, Madison appointed Monroe as his Secretary of State.

This diplomatic role required Monroe to focus once again on foreign relations, primarily with Britain and France. At this point, the French and British were at war with each other once again, which necessitated a delicate balance in relations with both countries as an objective third party.

Chapter 7 – The War of 1812

Tensions between America and Britain continued to escalate, largely due to the animosity between Britain and France.

At the time, Britain had the largest navy in the world and was actively blockading several French ports. The navy was also tasked with maintaining a military presence around their other colonies in the British Empire.

To meet the demands, Britain increased their fleet to 170 ships, but with limited manpower, Britain attacked American ships and forced their sailors aboard. This impressment had been a growing concern, and was now escalating toward a dangerous tipping point.

At the same time, Britain was trying to prevent America from trading with France, while France was doing the same. America, with a much smaller fleet, tried to stay neutral and not side with either country.

However, neither France nor Britain viewed the United States as a neutral country and both targeted America's trade practices. The primary offender, though, in the newer country's eyes, was Britain for its tendency toward impressment, which was responsible for capturing between 5,000 and 9,000 American sailors in less than a decade.

One of the most notorious examples of British impressment was with what is known as the Chesapeake Affair. Taking place off of the coast of Norfolk, the British warship HMS Leopard clashed with the USS Chesapeake, an American frigate. The Leopard pursued and attacked the Chesapeake.

Leopold commander Salusbury Humphreys ordered the removal of four crew from the Chesapeake after her commander, James Barron, surrendered after firing one shot. The men were tried for desertion and one was hanged. The others were sentenced to 500 lashings, but their sentences were later commuted.

Monroe intervened once more and negotiated the release of the captives. However, the British impressment actions continued, which heightened tensions between the two countries.

On top of that, the Americans suspected that Britain was behind riling up the Native Americans in the country and providing the supplies for carrying out raids against the colonists. If the British could be instrumental in allying with the Native Americans and pushing back the Americans, a neutral Native American state could be created to serve as a barrier between the U.S and Britain's interests in Canada.

Some people were clamoring for war once more. "War Hawks" Henry Clay and John C. Calhoun started making the case, along with new Congressmen.

For the most part, the Congressman from the South and the West were in support of the war, but those from New England, who depended on trade with Britain—or lack thereof by this point—opposed the warmongering.

Perhaps if the treaty that Jefferson had rejected had instead been passed, the relationship with Britain wouldn't have deteriorated to this point. However, there was no looking back for Monroe, and he instead focused his efforts as Secretary of State on how to best protect American's interests.

On June 18, 1812, with Monroe's support, President Madison officially signed a declaration of war against Britain, kicking off the War of 1812.

There were several battles over the next few years, but America still had comparatively fewer troops than Britain. To their benefit, though, British focus was split between the pesky Americans and fighting the war against Napoleon. During the first few years of the war, Monroe was instrumental in fortifying the military presence in Florida.

Beyond these efforts, Monroe was focusing his own efforts where needed and was serving in any way that he could to support his country. With his military history, he tried to give advice to the Secretary of War, John Armstrong, an attempt that Armstrong wholeheartedly rejected.

With the effective defeat of French troops in 1814, the British were immediately able to redouble their efforts and send more troops to America to fight. Still, Armstrong minimized the British capabilities, which would prove to be a bad military decision. While he was effectively turning his back on the British threat, Monroe often joined local troops who were patrolling the coast for signs of a growing threat.

Monroe wanted to return to battle, but Jefferson gently rebuked the efforts. Finally, when British troops were closing around the Americans in the Chesapeake Bay, he tasked himself with changing the troop deployment at Bladensburg. Brigadier General Tobias Stansbury had formed three lines of men, but Monroe repositioned them, inadvertently spreading them too far apart.

The British broke through the lines and then moved on to Washington, D.C. On August 24, 1814, the British burned several governmental buildings. In retaliation for the Americans attacking York in Ontario, they then turned their attention to the White House.

Fortunately, Madison and his wife were not in residence. The president, having ridden to meet with troops the previous day, told his wife to be on alert. If she saw signs of an attack, he instructed her to gather important papers and flee.

She managed to make it out in time, but not before securing a large portrait of George Washington. One can only imagine their collective relief when they finally met up with each other at a predetermined meeting place!

Their concerns were not unfounded and the British troops first ransacked the White House and then set it on fire, destroying the structure and further bruising the spirit of the American people.

While some members of Congress wanted the White House moved to a different location within Washington, or a different city altogether, Madison moved quickly to have reconstruction commence before a decision to move the location could be finalized.

Madison called in the original architect, James Hoban, to rebuild the executive mansion according to the original plans, but urged a quicker timeline in the rebuilding. In fact, while the first White House was built in 10 years, the replacement was constructed in three years' time.

Deeply disappointed in Secretary of War Armstrong's refusal to heed warnings about troops marching on Washington, Madison removed him from his position. Armstrong was quick to note that Monroe's actions may have led to the British breaking through their lines, but Madison was insistent in his removal.

Following on the heels of Armstrong's dismissal, Monroe was named the new Secretary of War. For the first time, one person held both the Secretary of State and the Secretary of War positions.

The tide of the war turned a year after his appointment as the Secretary of War. September 11, 1814, saw the Battle of Plattsburg Bay on Lake Champlain. This turning point ushered in a new peace treaty between American and British advisories. The Treaty of Ghent was signed on Christmas Eve of that year, signaling the end of the war.

Unfortunately, news traveled quite slowly at that time and it took nearly two months after the treaty was signed in Belgium to reach parts of the United States. By then, the Battle of New Orleans had already been executed and deemed a victory by the Americans.

Although the odds were stacked against the Americans in this battle, determined leadership by Major General Andrew Jackson and a successful conglomeration of U.S. soldiers, Choctaw tribesmen, free blacks and city aristocrats saw tremendous success for the defending party.

There were an estimated 100 American casualties to Britain's 2,000 wounded and killed. Jackson, nicknamed "Old Hickory" for his unwavering toughness, was escalated to high esteem and Monroe would later lavish praise on the war hero by saying, "History records no example of so glorious a victory obtained with so little bloodshed on the part of the victorious."

A month after news of the tremendous victory in the Battle of New Orleans reached the east coast, the news of the Treaty of Ghent finally crossed the ocean as well.

The treaty did not address two of the most pressing issues that brought the war—British impressment and recognizing the neutrality of U.S. vessels—the treaty did make room for expansion into the Great Lakes region, and was considered a diplomatic victory.

Chapter 8 – The Fifth President

James Monroe's wartime leadership bolstered confidence in his ability to succeed Madison as president in the 1816 elections. This time, the odds were much more in his favor.

While America could not claim victory over the War of 1812, the government and military did demonstrate to the American people that once again, it could push off its oppressors. The fact that the political party Monroe and Madison belonged to, the Democratic-Republican party, was in support of the war gave them the necessary credibility to launch another successful presidential bid.

The Federalist party, on the other hand, loudly opposed the war, which partly led to the party's later collapse. As it was, the Democratic-Republican party had already made concessions toward Federalist practices and policies, including tariffs to protect national interest as well as creating a national bank. This heightened Monroe's political party even more in the eyes of their supporters.

His opponents in the caucus were New York Governor Daniel D. Tompkins and William H. Crawford, Secretary of the Treasury. Crawford later deferred to Monroe, hoping to promote himself as a possible successor, and Monroe beat Tompkins to secure his name on the ballot, with Tompkins in position as his Vice President.

Monroe's political opponent was Rufus King, the man he replaced as ambassador to Great Britain in 1803, but there were not many people who backed the Federalist party or its nominee at that point.

When the votes were counted, James Monroe secured 183 of the 217 electoral votes, beating out King by a landslide. In fact, Monroe won all states except for Connecticut, Delaware and Massachusetts.

When he was inaugurated on March 4, 1817, the warm, sunny day matched the optimistic climate. At noon, the temperature was about 50 degrees, marking a beautiful day for the inaugural speech to be held outdoors.

Originally, the inauguration was slated to be held inside in the Capitol, in the House chamber. However, a heated debate ensued between the House of Representatives and the Senate about which chairs would be used for the event—the Senate wanted their gold-painted chairs to be used for the event.

In retrospect, it was beneficial that the oath of office took place outside because it allowed a large crowd estimated between 5,000 and 8,000 to bear witness.

Consequently, they decided to chance the winter weather and hold the inauguration on a temporary stage in front of the building, which was serving as the temporary Capital after the British invasion.

His speech started out humbly, showing his gratitude for the honor of serving the American people as their President. "I should be destitute of feeling if I was not deeply affected by the strong proof which my fellow-citizens have given me of their confidence in calling me to the high office whose functions I am about to assume," he said.

Standing in front of the Old Brick Capitol, which was serving as the temporary capitol after the British invasion, his speech enthusiastically moved to an upbeat tone. "During a period fraught with difficulties and marked by very extraordinary events the United States have flourished beyond example," he said. "Their citizens individually have been happy and the nation prosperous."

Interestingly, Monroe used the words "happy" or "happiness" nine times in his speech. It was not because he lacked a thesaurus, but he truly felt the positivity as surely as one feels the sun on his face.

And why not? The country had just thrown off an enemy country once more, and the country had ample room to grow.

"Fortunate as we are in our political institutions, we have not been less so in other circumstances on which our prosperity and happiness essentially depend," he said. "Situated within the temperate zone, and extending through many degrees of latitude along the Atlantic, the United States enjoy all the varieties of climate, and every production incident to that portion of the globe. Penetrating internally to the Great Lakes and beyond the sources of the great rivers which communicate through our whole interior, no country was ever happier with respect to its domain. Blessed, too, with a fertile soil, our produce has always been very abundant, leaving, even in years the least favorable, a surplus for the wants of our fellow-men in other countries."

Within the speech were words of warning, though; warning of what the country could become. "It is only when the people become ignorant and corrupt, when they degenerate into a populace, that they are incapable of exercising the sovereignty. Usurpation is then an easy attainment, and an usurper soon found. The people themselves become the willing instruments of their own debasement and ruin. Let us, then, look to the great cause, and endeavor to preserve it in full force. Let us by all wise and constitutional measures promote intelligence among the people as the best means of preserving our liberties."

Also, he suggested that the peace they had at the time may be temporary. "Dangers from abroad are not less deserving of attention. Experiencing the fortune of other nations, the United States may be again involved in war, and it may in that event be the object of the adverse party to overset our Government, to break our Union, and demolish us as a nation. Our distance from Europe and the just, moderate, and pacific policy of our Government may form some security against these dangers, but they ought to be anticipated and guarded against."

Monroe, with his wartime experience, was already anticipating what might happen. "To secure us against these dangers our coast and inland frontiers should be fortified, our Army and Navy, regulated upon just principles as to the force of each, be kept in perfect order, and our militia be placed on the best practicable footing."

While he went on to discuss fortifications and other suggestions, he also emphasized the importance of building and maintaining the country's infrastructure. "Other interests of high importance will claim attention, among which the improvement of our country by roads and canals, proceeding always with a constitutional sanction, holds a distinguished place. ... Nature has done so much for us by intersecting the country with so many great rivers, bays, and lakes, approaching from distant points so near to each other, that the inducement to complete the work seems to be peculiarly strong."

At the end of his speech, his tone turned humble once more. "In the Administrations of the illustrious men who have preceded me in this high station, with some of whom I have been connected by the closest ties from early life, examples are presented which will always be found highly instructive and useful to their successors." But his focus was not only his past experience; to be successful as president, he needed the support of other officials.

"Relying on the aid to be derived from the other departments of the Government," Monroe concluded, "I enter on the trust to which I have been called by the suffrages of my fellow-citizens with my fervent prayers to the Almighty that He will be graciously pleased to continue to us that protection which He has already so conspicuously displayed in our favor."

With the troubles of the country now being laid on his shoulders, Monroe also felt the tug of family commitments, particularly with his wife, Elizabeth. It is likely that her health was starting to fade at this point. While no official records are pinpointing her particular ailment, many people theorize that she had epilepsy.

Interestingly, while Monroe's wife was once held precious by the French when he served as the ambassador, the new role as First Lady proved a more difficult transition. Following in the footsteps of the vivacious former First Lady, Dolley Madison, Elizabeth was considered more aloof and standoffish. It is ironic that she was considered one of the most beautiful women in her generation and at 48 years old when Monroe took the office, her youthful appearance likely made her failing health more improbable in society's eyes and rumors started to circulate that she may be suffering from mental illness.

At the same time, Elizabeth also adopted the more European custom of stepping away from social obligations, bringing many of the social policies Dolley had enacted to a screeching halt.

Even though the inaugural reception was held at the Monroe's home on I Street, she was not present at his swearing-in, and was absent during the reception at their home.

On the holiday when patriotism reigned high, July 4, Elizabeth chose to spend the time in Virginia instead of being on hand for the annual Independence Day festivities. Because of this, many of Washington's society chose to boycott Administration receptions.

She neglected to make social calls, and many of Washington's society felt slighted, to the point that it became a topic of discussion at a cabinet meeting in December 1817.

While Elizabeth had withdrawn from the social spotlight, she did throw her efforts into decorating the White House. It had been built in three years, but it still lacked the furnishings worthy of a presidential family. Some say that Elizabeth tapped into her experiences in Europe to furnish the house; others claim Monroe made the choices himself and then deferred to Elizabeth. However, most agree that the Monroes tapped into their own finances to help with the furnishings, further pushing the family into the great crevasse of debt that the president would spend years trying to escape.

Chapter 9 – First Presidential Tour

Monroe's optimistic presence during his inauguration was extended through the early months of his tenure as President as he took the show on the road, so to speak, to meet with the people who elected him and to help build national trust.

After leaving Washington, D.C., on May 31, 1817, his first stop was in the Baltimore area, where one of his goals was to inspect Fort McHenry. The *Baltimore Patriot* captured the respect of the troops. "Although it was rather the wish of the President to perform his present tour without receiving any public demonstration of respect, the heads of the war and navy departments have, very properly, conceived it incompatible with all usage, and derogatory to the high office he holds, to wave the accustomary military and naval honors on his visit to the different posts and stations."

Upon leaving Baltimore, he elected to travel by steamboat, a rather hazardous decision, as the boats did not have high safety ratings at the time. In one estimate of the boats' dangers, there were explosions in one out of every five that took to the water between the years of 1811 to 1851.

Next, he traveled to Frenchtown, Maryland, and then Newcastle, Delaware. Here he and his traveling companions took a barge to Fort Mifflin.

Monroe spent a few days in early July in Philadelphia, visiting a number of different buildings and inspecting a Revolutionary War battleground, before taking a horse and traveling through New Jersey.

A June 12, 1817, newspaper article from the New Brunswick, New Jersey, *Fredonian* had nothing but glowing reports of Monroe's character. "All considerations of party were merged in the general wish to honor the man of the people—the dignified, yet affable—the illustrious, yet unassuming President," the article read. "No one can become acquainted with President Monroe, without being enamored of his simplicity; warmed by his engaging deportment; and charmed by his unaffected conversation."

In mid-June, Monroe spent more than a week in the New York City area, inspecting military structures, visiting hospitals and even a prison in the area.

Once again, the President took to the steamboat, this time on the *Connecticut*. He spent several days in the New London and Hartford, Connecticut, area. Even his clothing of choice received comments and compliments as it was a subtle throwback to his participation in the Revolutionary War.

"The Dress of the President has been deservedly noticed in other papers for its neatness and republican simplicity," wrote the *Connecticut Herald* in its June 9, 1817, issue. "He wore a plain blue coat, a buff under dress, and a hat and cockade of the revolutionary fashion. It comported with his rank, was adapted to the occasion, and well calculated to excite in the minds of the people, the remembrance of the day which 'tried men's souls.'"

Sadly, the tour wasn't without its issues. According to a July 8 edition of the Salem *Gazette*, one presidential salute in Pawtucket, of which there were many during Monroe's tour, badly injured a man in a cannon discharge. As a result of the accident, Smith Slocum had to have his arms amputated above the elbows because they were so badly damaged.

It was on his next major stop where the famous nickname for Monroe's early presidential administration was coined. "The Era of

Good Feelings" has often been credited as being named here. He timed his visit for so that he could be in Boston during the July 4 celebrations.

Based on the extensive newspaper articles and extensive diary entries, his stay in the Boston area was hardly a relaxing one. Not only did he visit the naval yard and toured ships and military arsenals, he also took in several gardens and made appearances at no less than 16 separate households—all in five days.

One of those stops in the Boston area was in Quincy, where Monroe paid a call to John Adams at his mansion.

Monroe's tour even took him as far north as what is now known as Maine, although the area was still a part of the state of Massachusetts at that point. He traveled as far north as Portland, Maine, receiving tremendous cheering and participating in animated conversations.

One can only imagine how touched he was when he entered Scarborough, Maine, passing under an archway of greenery and roses, which read, "UNITED WE STAND." When he arrived at the archway, Monroe left his carriage and walked under the greens.

According to a written recollection from Isaac Adams, chairman of the committee to welcome the president, "A living Eagle, a native of our own forests and the symbol of our martial prowess, perched on the summit of the twentieth arch, and under the canopy of stars, by which it was surmounted, apparently watching, with intense curiosity and surprise, the concourse of people passing under him, heightened in the bosom of every beholder, the interest of this lovely spectacle."

"It was a delightful sight to behold this haughty monarch of the feathered tribe, the pride of the forest, encircled by the blaze of the stars that he loves, stifling, for a moment, his untamed spirit of liberty; and gratefully spreading his pinions, as the chief of the nation passed, which had chosen him the whole range of animated nature, as the emblem of its glory and strength."

On July 17, President Monroe left the Maine territory and reentered New Hampshire, where local dignitaries escorted him through Dover, Rochester and Milton.

In Concord, committee chairman Thomas W. Thompson spoke of the optimism for more cohesiveness with the citizens of the United States. "Upon this auspicious occasion, party feelings are forever buried—and buried, we would hope, forever. A new era, we trust, is commencing."

The President passed into Vermont on July 23. Not only was he treated with the same respect, and returned it with a humble conversation, but he also spoke of the lush greenery the state was known for. One account while Monroe was on the banks of the Connecticut River, noted that, "The President, although born in the fertile regions of the South, could not suppress his admiration at the flourishing and productive state of the country upon this river."

In response, Monroe said in his speech, "I have approached the state of Vermont with peculiar sensibility. On a former visit, immediately after the war, I left a wilderness, and I now find it blooming with luxuriant promise of wealth and happiness, to a numerous population."

While in the area, he spoke with students of the Windsor Female Academy, telling them, "I take a deep interest as a parent and citizen, in the success of female education, and have been delighted, wherever I have been, to witness the attention paid to it."

After leaving Windsor, the entourage passed through Woodstock and Montpelier, before coming to Burlington, on the shores of Lake Champlain. Although the lake is smaller in comparison to the Great Lakes, Monroe understood the significance of the fortifications with the lake and passionately recalled its importance as a turning point in the War of 1812.

"The eventful action on your lake and its invaded shores," he said, "can never be contemplated without the deepest emotion. It bound the union by stronger ties, if possible, than ever."

Monroe moved on to speak of the exposure of the frontier areas and pledged to support them. "You may feel assured that the government will not withhold any practicable measures, for the security of your town; nor have I ever doubted that preparation for defense in time of peace, would ever prove the best economy for war."

On the western shores of Lake Champlain, he was met by citizens of Plattsburgh, New York, who focused on the vulnerability of living where they did. In turn, Monroe assured them that after the war's conclusion, the United States took steps to convince that British that "we had every reason to look for a permanent peace."

When Monroe arrived at Sackett's Harbor, one of the first areas the British tried to invade in the War of 1812, he met with several veterans of the Revolutionary War. In their address to the President, the men said collectively, "It is with pleasure that we, a few of the survivors of the revolution, residing in this part of the country, welcome the arrival of the chief magistrate of the union. It is with increased satisfaction we recognize in him one of the number engaged with us in the arduous struggle of establishing the independence of the country."

"We have lived, sir, to see the fruits of our toils and struggles amply realized in the happiness and prosperity of our country, and Sir, we have the fullest confidence, that under your administration, they will be handed down to our posterity unimpaired."

He traveled west even further, stopping over at Niagara Falls and meeting with the citizens of Buffalo, and then Detroit. Both areas had fallen victim to the British propensity for fires, but were slowly rebuilding.

In Detroit, he acknowledged their remote part of the territory, and urged the citizens to be ready for any further acts of aggression. "Aware of your exposed situation, every circumstance material to your defense in the possible, but I hope, remote contingency of future wars, has a just claim to, and will receive my attention. For any information which you maybe able to give me, on a subject of such high importance, I shall be very thankful.

"Your establishment was of necessity, in its origin, colonial; but on a new principle," he continued. "A parental hand cherishes you in your infancy."

It was time to turn the corner and start for home.

After his stop in Detroit, Monroe proceeded through Ohio, a state which only 50 years before was fully wild and barely touched by settlers. Philemon Beecher, chairman of the committee in Lancaster, Ohio, commented on their state's interest in following Monroe's tour to date. While they welcomed him wholeheartedly, they appeared somewhat embarrassed in their modest environs.

"If in your reception here," Beecher said, "we cannot, from the infant state of this part of the Union, exhibit the highest refinements of the most polished society, we flatter ourselves that the offerings of the West are accompanied with the warm and honest feeling of our honour thus voluntarily done us; and with the affection for him, who in this season of examination, has not overlooked us."

After Monroe departed from Lancaster, he traveled through Delaware and Columbus, Ohio. He received a reception in Chillicothe, Ohio, that was similar to the reception in Lancaster, but there was an additional layer of pride in Chillicothe Mayor Levin Belt's address to Monroe.

"The progress of the arts and sciences has not reached, in our state, the height of which they possess in some of our sister states," Belt said, "but our love of country and devotedness to her welfare is not surpassed by any."

Monroe later met with citizens of Zanesville and Putnam, Ohio, where he once again was greeted with a lengthy speech, to which Monroe responded with an equally verbose speech. He impressed upon them the fact that, while he was happy to meet the citizens of the country he now governed, they should not forget that he is a fellow citizen as well.

On September 5, Monroe toured Jefferson College in Canonsburg, Pennsylvania, where an address to Monroe expounded on the qualities of the institution. "We have ever viewed sound morality and intelligence as the great supports of free government, and the principal guarantee of our rights and privileges, both civil and religious."

In response to this speech, Monroe upheld the qualities of virtue and religion and complimented the college for its efforts to educate students with these things in mind.

In part of his speech, Monroe said, "Educated in these principles, we can, with confidence, repose our free government and the interests of our beloved country in their care, assured that they will preserve, protect, and cherish them, with equal honor and advantage."

Later that day, Monroe arrived in Pittsburgh. The next morning, he met with Pittsburgh's representatives and gave a recap of his experiences thus far on his tour. "I have seen, with great interest, in this Tour, the most satisfactory proofs of the rapid growth of this portion of our union; of the industry of its inhabitants; and in their progress of agriculture, manufactures, and the useful arts."

There, at the junction of the Monongahela and Allegheny rivers, Monroe took pride in mentioning his success in securing New Orleans, nearly 2,000 miles away, allowing for secure passage without the threat of foreign barriers.

After leaving Pittsburgh, the pace of the tour picked up as Monroe headed back to Washington, D.C. Within a week of fast travel and hard riding, the group reached Fredericktown, Maryland, and proceeded to the capital city.

The people of Washington, D.C. greeted him with enthusiastic joy upon his arrival on September 17. The vacuum created when he went on his tour three months before was finally filled once more.

Benjamin Orr, Mayor of Washington, D.C., represented the sentiment of many in the nation's capital when he spoke to Monroe the next morning. "Mr. President," he said, "In the tour which you have just finished, we have sympathized with you in your fatigues, and exulted with you in the extraordinary demonstrations of the nation's love, which, though sometimes oppressive, are always grateful."

Monroe's pleasure as he recalled his tour was evident in his response. "I shall always look back to the important incidents of my late Tour with particular satisfaction. I flatter myself that I have derived from it information which will be very useful in the discharge of duties in the high trust confided to me; and in other respects, it has afforded me the greatest gratification."

"In all that portion of our country, through which I have passed, I have seen, with delight, proofs of the most conclusive, of the devotion of our fellow citizens to the principles of our free republican government, and to our happy union. The spontaneous and independent manner of which these sentiments were declared, by the great body of the people, with other marked circumstances attending them, satisfied me that they came from the heart."

It was time to return his focus to matters of running the country, such as appointing his cabinet. Secretary of War John Calhoun was from South Carolina and Benjamin Crowningshield hailed from Massachusetts. Crowningshield was appointed as the Secretary of the Navy. The two were part of a geographically balanced cabinet, along with the recently appointed Richard Rush of Pennsylvania and Massachusetts resident John Quincy Adams.

The following year, he would take to the road again to tour other parts of the United States.

Chapter 10 – Second Presidential Tour

Monroe's first tour to the north afforded him the time and ability to meet with citizens, inspect military installations and devise a plan to defend the frontier and areas exposed to the Atlantic Ocean. Conversely, his second tour was much shorter, and took him to the Chesapeake Bay area.

The tour kicked off after Congress adjourned its 1817-1818 session. On this tour was his Secretary of War and Secretary of the Navy. Near the end of May 1818, Monroe and his group departed from Washington, D.C. One of their first stops was Annapolis, where Monroe lived in 1793 and peace negotiations commenced after the Revolutionary War.

Annapolis Mayor John Randall recalled the atmosphere of Maryland's capital city at the time that Monroe resided there. "The rigor of the season at that time was unfavorable to a view of the situation of the place and its surrounding waters, the prospect of which is now expanding and embellished by the military establishments erected by the United States, which of course will come into your observation."

In turn, Monroe's speech also recalled those events. "In recurring to the period of 1783, when Congress was held their session here, you bring to view, incidence of the highest degree important. It was then, and here, after a long and arduous struggle, which secured our independence, that the Treaty of Peace was ratified. It was then, and here, but the lustrous commander of our revolutionary armies, after performing Services, of which a grateful country can never forget, nor time obliterate, restored his commission to the authority with whom he had received it. To me these events... were particularly imposing an impressive. It was then, in very early life, that I commenced my career in the National Council, and which I have since so long continued. To me again, so many of those who were present at those great events, some of home, were parties to them, affords me the greatest gratification."

After leaving Annapolis, Monroe spent quite a bit of time touring the Chesapeake Bay area, which, at the time was the largest bay in the country. Monroe examined all facets of the bay, strategizing the best way to defend it, should war again come to America's shores.

On June 7, 1818, Monroe arrived in Norfolk, Virginia, where he was greeted by dignitaries. Mayor John Holt spoke: "The personal attention, sir, which you have thought proper to bestow on measures adopted by the general government, for the defense of our Inland Frontier, and Seacoast, and the establishment of naval arsenals, confidently assures us, our country will reap the full benefit of these measures from your extended observation, practical knowledge, and judicious discrimination."

Monroe assured the people of Norfolk in his return address that they would be well defended. "No object is more interesting to the United States than the adoption of a judicious system of defense, and the establishment and construction of such fortifications as may be found necessary for the security of our Maritime and Inland Frontier. Such a system, well-executed, may prevent wars, and it cannot fail, should war become inevitable, to mitigate their calamities."

After spending some more time in Virginia, Monroe returned to Washington, D.C., on June 17, 1818.

Several months later, when addressing Congress once more, Monroe concluded respectfully to God. "When we view the greater blessings with which our country has been favored, those which we now enjoy, and the means by which we possess of handing them down unimpaired, to our latest posterity, our attention is irresistibly drawn to the source from whence they flow. Let us, then, unite and offering our most grateful acknowledgments for these blessings to the Divine Author of all good."

First Lady Elizabeth Monroe maintained her departure from society, often relying on her eldest, Eliza, who was by then married to prominent attorney George Hay. Eliza had been educated in French schools, including one headed by Madame Campan, who served as Marie Antoinette's lady in waiting.

While Eliza upheld Elizabeth's nod toward social exclusivity, the Monroe daughter did cultivate many politically strong relationships, such as Hortense de Beauharnais, and Caroline Bonaparte, who respectively became Queen of Holland and Queen of Naples.

And while she was often seen as standoffish, Louisa Catherine Adams, wife to James Quincy Adams, appeared a staunch supporter of Elizabeth, speaking of her in effusive, complimentary terms. "The Drawing room was full tho' not crowded and we had altogether a very pleasant evening. Mrs. Monroe as usual looked beautiful," Louisa wrote in her diary.

And, in a letter to John Adams after an encounter with Elizabeth, Louisa wrote, "She was dressed in white and gold made in the highest style of fashion and moved not like a Queen (for that is an unpardonable word in this country) but like a goddess."

Chapter 11 – The Era of Good Feelings Challenged

With his two lengthy tours behind him, Monroe settled into the challenges that would later define his presidency.

In 1817, determined to improve relations with Britain once again, Monroe was determined to oversee demilitarization in the Great Lakes area. On April 16, 1818, the Senate ratified the Rush–Bagot Treaty between the United States and Britain, limiting both countries to one military vessel and one cannon on Lake Ontario and Lake Champlain. These countries were also permitted two military vessels on the remaining Great Lakes.

In what was considered the largest demilitarized zone, the treaty resulted in 5,527 miles of the east-west boundary.

"I have the satisfaction to inform you that an arrangement which had been commenced by my predecessor with the British Government for the reduction of the naval force by Great Britain and the United States on the Lakes has been concluded," Monroe said triumphantly. "By this arrangement useless expense on both sides and, what is of still greater importance, the danger of collision between armed vessels in those inland waters, which was great, is prevented."

The Florida territory, under Spanish rule, was starting to become a problem for the United States. Not only was Spain proving to be an absentee parent, but skirmishes with the Native Americans in the area were requiring the attention of the United States military once more.

General Andrew Jackson was called on to march into Florida with 4,000 troops. Seizing the fort in St. Augustine, he discovered illegal slave trading, and troublesome gun sales to the Native Americans there.

Additionally, it was common practice for slaves who escaped their masters to hide out in Florida, gaining sanctuary from Seminole and Creek tribes.

Congress was worried that this might be perceived as a threat to Spain, and some demanded that Adams be removed from his position, but Monroe defended the move in Florida. "Spain had lost her authority over it," he said. "And, falling into the hands of adventurers connected with the savages, it was made the means of unceasing annoyance and our Union in many of its most essential interests."

Secretary of State John Quincy Adams was called in to tenderly negotiate the purchase of Florida. He stressed that Florida was "a derelict open to the occupancy of every enemy, civilized or savage, of the United States, and serving no other earthly purpose than as a post of annoyance to them."

The Adams-Onis Treaty was signed on February 22, 1819, by Adams and Luis de Onís, Spanish minister, and two years later, the eastern part of Florida was turned over to the United States. "By this cession, then, Spain ceded a territory in reality of no value to her," Monroe concluded.

There was no money exchanged in the sale, but it did agree to pay legal claims of Americans against Spain for as much as $5 million. In fact, there were 1,859 claims from more than 720 incidents, which were handled by Daniel Webster and William Wirt, as well as other attorneys.

In addition, the United States gave up any claim to the Texas territory, for the time being.

Tensions with Spain were put to rest with the treaty but the problems were far from over for Monroe.

In 1819, the first major depression struck since the constitution was ratified. Known as the Panic of 1819, the economy began to collapse as the global economy adjusted itself after the Napoleonic Wars.

Additionally, westward expansion and real estate speculation demanded increased credit extended by the Second Bank of the United States. The resulting effects were widespread. People were thrown into debtors' prisons, land was devalued and dropped from an estimated $70 an acre to $2 per acre, unemployment rose and countless banks were bankrupt.

People turned against Monroe for not doing enough to prevent the depression. Although Monroe was convinced that this was a normal part of any economy, he did press Secretary of Treasury William Crawford to relax mortgage payments on land purchased from the United States itself.

The depression ended officially in 1823, but there were other problems Monroe was facing.

In February 1820, the Missouri territory sought to join the Union as a state and a bill was put together and submitted to the House of Representatives. It was then that Congressman James Tallmadge, Jr. offered the Tallmadge Amendment.

The amendment, if passed, would prohibit more slaves from being introduced into Missouri. It also stated that all future children of slave parents would be freed when they turned 25 years old.

Three days later, the bill passed in the House of Representatives, but those amendments were then rejected in the Senate and in December 1819, Alabama was allowed into the union as a slave state. At this point, the number of free states and slave states were equal.

In January 26, 1820, the House of Representatives passed a similar bill introduced by New York's John W. Taylor, which allowed Missouri into the Union as a slave state, at the same time that a bill was introduced to admit Maine as a free state. At that point, in February, the Senate decided to put the two ideas together and passed a bill allowing Maine in while also allowing Missouri to enter into the union as a slave state.

Monroe was deeply affected by the impact of the compromise. In his personal notes found, he wrote in February, "The idea was that if the whole arrangement, to this effect, could be secured, that it would be better to adopt it, than break the union. Neither did Mr. Barbour, nor any other person alluded to, favor this, but to save the union, believing it to be in imminent danger."

Others were acutely aware of Monroe's concerns, and the next month, John Henry Eaton wrote to Jackson on behalf of the president. "The agitation was indeed great I assure you," Eaton wrote. "Dissolution of the Union had become quite a familiar subject. By the compromise however restricting slavery north of 36½ degrees we ended this unpleasant question. Of this the Southern people are complaining, but they ought not, for it has preserved peace, dissipated angry feelings, and dispelled appearances which seemed dark and horrible and threatening to the interest and harmony of the nation. The constitution has not been surrendered by this peace offering, for it only applies while a territory when it is admitted congress have the power and right to legislate, and not when they shall become States."

On March 6, the President signed the compromise, but the discussion was far from over. In fact, the debate continued throughout the nation.

In April, Jefferson wrote to John Homes. "I had for a long time ceased to read newspapers or pay any attention to public affairs, confident they were in good hands, and content to be a passenger in our bark to the shore from which I am not distant. but this momentous question, like a fire bell in the night, awakened and filled me with terror. I considered it at once as the knell of the Union. it is hushed indeed for the moment, but this is a reprieve only, not a final sentence."

"I perceive you have strong foreboding as to our future policy," Calhoun later wrote to Andrew Jackson in June 1820. "The discussion on the Missouri question has undoubtedly contributed to weaken in some degree the attachment of our southern and western people to the Union; but the agitators of that question have, in my opinion, not only completely failed; but have destroyed to a great extent their capacity for future mischief. Should Missouri be admitted at the next session, as I think she will without difficulty, the evil effects of the discussion must gradually subside."

Not all was dismal in the era though. Monroe's first term saw the wedding of his second daughter. Maria Hester Monroe became the first presidential child to be married in the White House. In March 9, 1820, Maria married Samuel L. Gouverneur, her first cousin and a White House staffer.

Although held at the White House, the wedding was very private. Only 42 close friends and family were invited to attend. Perhaps because of the backlash, the couple planned to attend several balls.

Nine days after Maria and Samuel were married, they attended their first ball at Stephen Decatur's house. During the ball, Decatur was challenged to a duel, which he accepted. Within that week, he was killed in the duel. Society fell into mourning and the upcoming festivities were canceled.

Chapter 12 – Reelection and Building the Country

James Monroe's first term was coming to a close and he was urged to seek another term. By this time, the Federalist party had completely collapsed, so there was so challenger and Monroe was the second president in United States history to run unopposed.

The electoral vote was not unanimous, however. William Plumer from Epping, New Hampshire, cast his vote for John Quincy Adams. Some of his opponents thought that he did this just to ensure that George Washington was the only president unanimously elected. The contention is a practical one—Plumer had so much respect for the first president that he named one of his six children George Washington Plumer.

However, Plumer emphatically stated that he submitted his vote in the Electoral College because he felt the president to be incompetent. When submitting his vote for Vice President, Plumer also voted against Monroe's running mate, Daniel D. Thompkins; instead, he cast his vote for Richard Rush.

Even John Adams, the man who had been part of founding the Federalist party, came out of retirement to cast his vote for Monroe.

Unlike his first inauguration, it was cold and snowy on Monday, March 5, a day after the inauguration was initially scheduled. This marked the first time the country was temporarily without a president since Washington took office, and after Monroe's first term expired at noon on March 4, Senate President Pro Tem John Gaillard took up the duty of President for a day.

Gaillard's duties were hardly taxing and the inauguration took place the next day in a snowbound capital after snow began on that Saturday.

At an estimated 28 degrees, as noted by John Quincy Adams, Monroe's second oath of office was made inside the House Chambers. However, the ceremony was a festive one and they were regaled by the Marine Corps Band in their first appearance in an official event, playing "Yankee Doodle Dandy" at the conclusion.

While his Vice President, Daniel Tompkins, was on hand during his first inauguration, he was in New York at the time of the 1821 inauguration and chose not to travel to Washington to be sworn in for the second time.

At first, the president was hesitant about making a speech, since it was actually not required by the Constitution. However, his advisors strongly suggested that he should make a speech. Rising to the occasion, he constructed a speech that was more than 4,400 words long and lasted for more than an hour.

There were concerns that the floor might buckle under the weight of the waterlogged spectators, but others were more concerned with staying awake through the entire speech.

Once again, Monroe started out with a humble tone. "I shall not attempt to describe the grateful emotions which the new and very distinguished proof of the confidence of my fellow-citizens, evinced by my reelection to this high trust, has excited in my bosom," he began in his speech.

Monroe also spoke about the economic struggles they were still encountering. "Our commerce had been in a great measure driven from the sea, our Atlantic and inland frontiers were invaded in almost every part; the waste of life along our coast and on some parts of our inland frontiers, to the defense of which our gallant and patriotic citizens were called, was immense, in addition to which not less than $120,000,000 were added at its end to the public debt."

However, he explained, it was imperative that the country remain a neutral global presence. "At the period adverted to the powers of Europe, after having been engaged in long and destructive wars with each other, had concluded a peace, which happily still exists. Our peace with the power with whom we had been engaged had also been concluded," he said. "Respecting the attitude which it may be proper for the United States to maintain hereafter between the parties, I have no hesitation in stating it as my opinion that the neutrality heretofore observed should still be adhered to," he stated, as impractical as it sounded. "Europe is again unsettled and the prospect of war increasing. Should the flame light up in any quarter, how far it may extend it is impossible to foresee. It is our peculiar felicity to be altogether unconnected with the causes which produce this menacing aspect elsewhere."

Domestically, though, neutrality may not have been possible. Monroe highlighted some of the struggles with the Native Americans. "The care of the Indian tribes within our limits has long been an essential part of our system, but, unfortunately, it has not been executed in a manner to accomplish all the objects intended by it. We have treated them as independent nations, without their having any substantial pretensions to that rank. The distinction has flattered their pride, retarded their improvement, and in many instances paved the way to their destruction." And while he seemed empathetic, he did not turn away from pushing the United States boundary ever west. "The progress of our settlements westward, supported as they are by a dense population, has constantly driven them back, with almost the total sacrifice of the lands which they have been compelled to abandon. They have claims on the magnanimity and, I may add, on the justice of this nation which we must all feel. We should become their real benefactors; we should perform the office of their Great Father, the endearing title which they emphatically give to the Chief Magistrate of our Union."

This time, Elizabeth was present at the swearing in.

Without the necessary time to transition into the executive mansion he already occupied, it was time to move on with his presidential duties.

With the addition of Missouri and Maine, the United States continued to grow and with that, the need for a better infrastructure was evident.

"When we consider the vast extent of territory within the United States," he said, "the great amount and value of its productions, the connection of its parts, and other circumstances on which their prosperity and happiness depend, we can not fail to entertain a high sense of the advantage to be derived from the facility which may be afforded in the intercourse between them by means of good roads and canals. Never did a country of such vast extent offer equal inducements to improvements of this kind, nor ever were consequences of such magnitude involved in them."

Monroe was concerned that the Constitution did not give the government the authority to construct or maintain a national transportation system and asked Congress to amend the Constitution.

However, Congress refused to make any amendments, deciding instead that it gave the government too much power.

In 1822, though, Congress passed a bill to make improvements on the Cumberland Road, also known as the National Road. The roadway ran from Wheeling, Virginia, to Cumberland, Maryland.

Monroe vetoed the bill on May 4. "It is with deep regret," he said in his veto message, "approving as I do the policy, that I am compelled to object to its passage and to return the bill to the House of Representatives, in which it originated, under a conviction that Congress do not possess the power under the Constitution to pass such a law."

"A power to establish turnpikes with gates and tolls, and to enforce the collection of tolls by penalties, implies a power to adopt and execute a complete system of internal improvement," he explained. "I am of opinion that Congress do not possess this power; that the States individually can not grant it, for although they may assent to the appropriation of money within their limits for such purposes, they can grant no power of jurisdiction or sovereignty by special compacts with the United States. This power can be granted only by an amendment to the Constitution and in the mode prescribed by it."

However, the issue was not dead and the President turned to the Supreme Court justices and others to discuss his concerns.

Two years after he vetoed the bill, Monroe signed a bill to fund surveys and estimates for the road. One year later, in 1825, he signed a bill to extend the road all the way to Zanesville, Ohio. On July 4 of that year, the ground was broken for the road in Ohio.

Now that national obligations were addressed, Monroe tackled foreign concerns. During this time, Latin American territories were attempting to remove themselves from Spain's grasp. With his own revolutionary experience, Monroe could certainly sympathize with his southern counterparts but he maintained the attempt at neutrality that he upheld and refused to side with either party.

However, when Argentina, Columbia, Chile, Peru and Mexico all won their independence from Spain, Monroe felt he could make an official move. In March 1822, Monroe instructed his Secretary of State to write instructions for the officials he would be sending to these countries as their ministers.

Despite his initial hesitancy, this move made the United States the first to officially recognize these countries, and set the stage for the rest of the world to follow.

Within the instructions Adams dictated, the United States declared that they would support Republican efforts, while also working toward treaties of commerce on the basis of what was known as the 'most favored nation.'

In the meantime, Spain and Britain were bristling for a fight. Britain wholeheartedly cheered Spain's looting these colonies, and the trade restrictions they might bring on.

Adding to the international tensions was Russia. Although Monroe said in his second inaugural speech that, "I have great satisfaction in stating that our relations with France, Russia, and other powers continue on the most friendly basis," Tsar Alexander was eyeballing expansion along the Pacific coast. After Russia defeated Napoleonic France, the tsar deemed himself the head of the Holy Alliance, a group of monarchs from Russia, Prussia and Austria who were dedicated to staunch liberalism and secular views.

In 1891, Tsar Alexander pronounced that the area north of the 51st parallel would be held for Russian interests only. In response, John Quincy Adams, once the first ambassador to Russia, refused to honor the claim as Secretary of State.

With the major world powers still in a state of flux, Adams and Monroe determined it was time to take a stand for American soil once and for all.

While the verbiage was encapsulated in his address to Congress on December 2, 1823, the message rang loud and clear to nations planning to capitalize on North American lands.

"At the proposal of the Russian Imperial Government, made through the minister of the Emperor residing here, a full power and instructions have been transmitted to the minister of the United States at St. Petersburg to arrange by amicable negotiation the respective rights and interests of the two nations on the northwest coast of this continent," Monroe said as he transitioned into what is now known as the Monroe Doctrine.

"A similar proposal has been made by His Imperial Majesty to the Government of Great Britain, which has likewise been acceded to. The Government of the United States has been desirous by this friendly proceeding of manifesting the great value which they have invariably attached to the friendship of the Emperor and their solicitude to cultivate the best understanding with his Government. In the discussions to which this interest has given rise and in the arrangements by which they may terminate the occasion has been judged proper for asserting, as a principle in which the rights and interests of the United States are involved, that the American continents, by the free and independent condition which they have assumed and maintain, are *henceforth not to be considered as subjects for future colonization by any European powers.*"

"It was stated at the commencement of the last session that a great effort was then making in Spain and Portugal to improve the condition of the people of those countries, and that it appeared to be conducted with extraordinary moderation. It need scarcely be remarked that the results have been so far very different from what was then anticipated. Of events in that quarter of the globe, with which we have so much intercourse and from which we derive our origin, we have always been anxious and interested spectators."

Once again, Monroe selected a word he often chose in his speeches: happy. "The citizens of the United States cherish sentiments the most friendly in favor of the liberty and happiness of their fellow-men on that side of the Atlantic."

The President spoke of the country's desire to remain neutral and would only take up arms to defend her lands. "In the wars of the European powers in matters relating to themselves we have never taken any part, nor does it comport with our policy to do so. It is only when our rights are invaded or seriously menaced that we resent injuries or make preparation for our defense."

And in turn for steadfast neutrality, Monroe said, the United States expected the same consideration on their soil. If this did not happen, there would be ramifications. "We owe it, therefore, to candor and to the amicable relations existing between the United States and those powers to declare that we should consider any attempt on their part to extend their system to any portion of this hemisphere as dangerous to our peace and safety. With the existing colonies or dependencies of any European power we have not interfered and shall not interfere. But with the Governments who have declared their independence and maintain it, and whose independence we have, on great consideration and on just principles, acknowledged, we could not view any interposition for the purpose of oppressing them, or controlling in any other manner their destiny, by any European power in any other light than as the manifestation of an unfriendly disposition toward the United States."

Monroe noted that Spain and Portugal remained unsettled and continued by saying, "Our policy in regard to Europe, which was adopted at an early stage of the wars which have so long agitated that quarter of the globe, nevertheless remains the same, which is, not to interfere in the internal concerns of any of its powers; to consider the government de facto as the legitimate government for us; to cultivate friendly relations with it, and to preserve those relations by a frank, firm, and manly policy, meeting in all instances the just claims of every power, submitting to injuries from none."

In other words, the President concluded that no country should get involved with matters of other countries. "It is still the true policy of the United States to leave the parties to themselves, in hope that other powers will pursue the same course."

The frank statement, which wasn't coined as the Monroe Doctrine until 1850, clearly drew a line in the sand. And while the young, feisty country may not have been able to ward off a full-on attack from another military powerhouse, by this time, the United States and Britain were once again on amicable terms. With Britain staunchly supporting the declaration, the United States could be confident in naval support from Britain should the need arise.

This has been considered the first significant policy issued by the United States in her defense and in support of the Western Hemisphere. To date, it has been referred to on a handful of occasions.

Of course, relations with Britain continued to wax and wane. In 1842, President John Tyler applied the Monroe Doctrine to warn their sometimes-allies off from Hawaii, as the United States began the process of taking the territory into her fold.

During the Mexican-American War, President James Polk enacted the Monroe Doctrine to annex what is now the state of Texas. After that, President Theodore Roosevelt utilized the policy to underscore the United States' presence in the Philippines as well as the Caribbean and Central America.

Perhaps the most widely known application of the Monroe Doctrine in recent history was in 1962, when President John F. Kennedy led the country in mitigating the Cuban Missile Crisis. No stranger to the doctrine, Kennedy also referred to it the previous year during the Bay of Pigs invasion. While the military action was short-lived, the United States was destined to tussle with Cuba's government the following year.

On October 16, 1962, Kennedy convened his Executive Committee after the country became aware of several nuclear missiles in Cuba. After much military discussion and maneuvering, the president addressed the country on October 22.

"This Government, as promised, has maintained the closest surveillance of the Soviet military buildup on the island of Cuba," Kennedy began in his speech. "Within the past week, unmistakable evidence has established the fact that a series of offensive missile sites is now in preparation on that imprisoned island. The purpose of these bases can be none other than to provide a nuclear strike capability against the Western Hemisphere."

A few days later, on October 29, the president was asked directly about the Monroe Doctrine in a news conference. He responded, "The Monroe Doctrine means what it has meant since President Monroe and John Quincy Adams enunciated it, and that is that we would oppose a foreign power extending its power to the Western Hemisphere. And that's why we oppose what is being--what's happening in Cuba today. That's why we have cut off our trade. That's why we worked in the OAS and in other ways to isolate the Communist menace in Cuba. That's why we'll continue to give a good deal of our effort and attention to it."

Known as a cornerstone of American policy, the Monroe Doctrine has proven to be a powerful tool in protecting the country from foreign threats.

A year after the Monroe Doctrine was released, Monroe invited his good friend Marquis de Lafayette to return to America. It was time, he thought, to instill the "spirit of 1776'" to the younger generation of Americans.

In a letter to Lafayette dated February 24, 1824, Monroe said, "I wrote you a letter about 15 days since, by Mr. Brown, in which I expressed the wish to send to any port in France should you point out, a frigate to convey you hither, in case you should be able to visit the United States. Since then, Congress has passed a resolution on the subject, and which sincere attachment of the whole nation to use expressed, whose ardent desire is once more to see you amongst them. At which you may yield to this invitation is left entirely at your option, but believe me, whatever may be your decision, it will be sufficient that you should have the goodness to inform me of it, and immediate orders will be given for a government vessel receipt for to any port you will indicate, and convey to you then the adopted country of your early youth, just always preserved the most grateful recollection of your important Services. I send to you herewith the resolution of Congress, and add thereto the assurance of my high consideration and of my sentiments of affection."

Despite Louis XVIII's disapproval of the trip, Lafayette departed French shores on July 13, 1824, and the Revolutionary War hero did indeed return to America with a full hero's welcome in New York City.

After several days in New York, Lafayette traveled to Boston where he was warmly greeted. "Greetings! Friend of our fathers!" boomed

Edward Everett, the politician who gave the "Other Gettysburg Address" before Lincoln's famous speech. "May you be welcome on our shores! Happy are our eyes to look upon your venerable features! Enjoy a triumph, which is reserved for neither conquerors nor monarchs, the assurance that here in all America there is not a heart which does not beat with joy and gratitude at the sound of your name."

In September of his great tour, Lafayette journeyed to the many of the same cities as Monroe did through his first presidential tour: New Haven, Connecticut; Providence, Rhode Island; Portsmouth, New Hampshire, Saco, Maine.

He then headed south, stopping in Washington, D.C., and then went on to Mount Vernon where he visited Washington's tomb. An emotional Lafayette, at Washington's final resting place, said, "The feelings, which on this awful moment oppress my heart don't leave me the power of utterance. I can only thank you, my dear Custis for your precious gift and pray a silent homage to the tomb of the greatest and best of men, my paternal friend."

Among his 13-month trip, Lafayette traveled through Louisiana, Mississippi, Georgia, South Carolina, North Carolina, Tennessee and Kentucky. During his trip to Louisville on the steamboat *Mechanic*, the ship sinks. While everyone reached shore safely, Lafayette lost both possessions and money.

He is also the guest of honor at the White House in early December. Even Elizabeth Monroe makes a rare public appearance at a reception in his honor.

By the time Lafayette boards the American warship, the *Brandywine*, to return home, John Quincy Adams is the next president.

Chapter 13 – Post Presidency

Following in the footsteps of his presidential predecessors, James Monroe decided not to run for a third term as president.

His eighth annual message as the President would be his final one. While steadfastly providing updates on the health of the country, his final words were bittersweet. "I can not conclude this communication, the last of the kind which I shall have to make, without recollecting with great sensibility and heartfelt gratitude the many instances of the public confidence and the generous support which I have received from my fellow citizens in the various trusts with which I have been honored. Having commenced my service in early youth, and continued it since with few and short intervals, I have witnessed the great difficulties to which our union has been surmounted. From the present prosperous and happy state I derive a gratification which I can not express. That these blessings may be preserved and perpetuated will be the object of my fervent and unceasing prayers to the Supreme Ruler of the Universe."

Monroe's presidency ended on March 4, 1825, when John Quincy Adams was sworn in as the sixth president of the United States.

In another presidential first, Monroe became the first presidential escort the President-Elect to the swearing-in ceremony. While the two rode in separate carriages, the strength of the party's unity and their own friendship could not be denied.

And, in another example of presidential camaraderie, the Monroes were permitted to remain in the White House for an additional three weeks, as Elizabeth had fallen ill and was too sick to leave the White House.

When she had recovered, the Monroes traveled to their home in Oak Hill, located in Loudoun County, Virginia.

After the presidential world, life settled into a quiet routine. Elizabeth focused her efforts on her family and the Monroe daughters often came to visit.

Supporting Jefferson's focus on the University of Virginia, James Monroe regularly attended Board of Visitors meetings and served as the rector for a time. He was also appointed to the Virginia Constitutional Convention and in 1829, he was asked to serve as the presiding officer.

However, his health was failing and he was forced to withdraw from his final civic duty.

Monroe also turned to writing, spending a considerable time penning a book that compared the current political clime to other nations, both ancient and modern. It may be the premise of this book that was inspired by Monroe's words: "If we look to the history of other nations, ancient or modern, we find no example of a growth so rapid, so gigantic, of a people so prosperous and happy."

However, as much as he wanted to write this book, it proved too much, so he chose another subject and began writing his autobiography. That would never come to fruition either.

Soon, tragedy struck. In 1826, Elizabeth became ill once more. Whether it was a weakness from her malady or an epileptic seizure, no one knows for sure. Sadly, she fell into an open fire and was severely burned.

In even more tenuous health circumstances, Monroe's beloved wife lived for three more years, often in considerable pain from her burns.

On September 23, 1830, Elizabeth passed away at the family home in Oak Hills. She was 62 years old.

Despondent, Monroe was said to have sat by the fire after her death and systematically fed page upon page of his private letters to and from Elizabeth into the fire. It is one of the reasons much less is known about the personal life of this President than most others of his status.

Elizabeth was interred at Oak Hills, a place Monroe himself left not long after. With his financial woes ever dogging him, he moved in with his daughter, Maria. Even then, the former President knew he would not live much longer.

His friend, John Quincy Adams visited him for the final time in 1831. The two men discussed the current affairs in Europe, but Adams opted to cut the visit short, afraid he was tiring Monroe.

About 3:30 p.m. on July 4, 1831, James Monroe, war hero, diplomat and fifth president died in New York City in his daughter's home, ten months after burying his wife. The official cause of death was heart failure and tuberculosis.

His death, 55 years after the Declaration of Independence was signed, made him the third President to die on what would later become known as Independence Day. One other President that died on July 4th was John Adams. His last recorded words were, "Thomas Jefferson still survives." But that was not to be, as Jefferson also died on July 4, 1826, 50 years to the day of the country's birthday.

The *Niles' Weekly Register* published James Monroe's obituary on July 23. "The body having been brought by a guard of honor from the late residence of the deceased, accompanied by intimate relatives and friends, was deposited on the platform in front of City Hall. Immediately above it, a temporary stage, covered with a black cloth, had been erected."

The funeral was held at St. Paul's Episcopal Church and was conducted by Rev. Bishop Onderdonk and Rev. Dr. Wainwright.

"The body was carried on a hearse, covered with black cloth, fringed with gold," the obituary continued. "From the centre panels, the national flag hung reversed, and eight black feathers waved above the whole; the hearse was drawn by four black horses."

Even after his death, poverty still reared its ugly head and he was buried in New York City with financial assistance. He was interred at Marble Cemetery, but this was not his final resting place.

In 1858, Madison's coffin was exhumed and prepared for transport back to his home state of Virginia. After it was briefly on display at City Hall in New York City, it was loaded onto a barge in preparation for the trip. Unfortunately, the transport encountered several storms, including one which swept a member of the honor guard—Alexander Hamilton's grandson—overboard.

Finally, he was reinterred at the President's Circle at Hollywood Cemetery in Richmond, Virginia. The remains of his beloved wife were also exhumed and reinterred to rest eternally beside him at Hollywood Cemetery.

Conclusion

James Monroe, the fifth President of the United States, is often overlooked as a President. However, as one of the Founding Fathers, his steadfast desire to promote and preserve America's interests, was evident in his many deeds and accomplishments.

When Monroe left the White House, he had served the interests of the United States for more than 50 years, both domestically and internationally. His political elections are said to eclipse any other President for the number of appointments he was given.

James B. Murray, Jr. attended the College of William and Mary centuries after Monroe was a student before the Revolutionary War. In 1995, Murray paid tribute to Monroe's legacy at a Charter Day ceremony.

"While Monroe may not be credited as a creator of this nation, he should be credited with being a builder of this nation," Murray said in his speech. "We all revere the history of the College. We feel the pride of it in our bones, yet our appreciation for the roots of that pride is often episodic. Too often we overlook the greater glory of having educated one of America's greatest presidents."

Had Monroe not persevered in supporting the United States, the country may be vastly different now, he said. "Occasionally we need reminding that so much we take for granted about our nation today was far from assured during those early years. It took a nation-building president to assure this nation."

Free Bonus from Captivating History (Available for a Limited time)

Hi History Lovers!

Now you have a chance to join our exclusive history list so you can get your first history ebook for free as well as discounts and a potential to get more history books for free! Simply visit the link below to join.

Captivatinghistory.com/ebook

Also, make sure to follow us on:

Twitter: @Captivhistory

Facebook: Captivating History:@captivatinghistory

Read more biographies from Captivating History

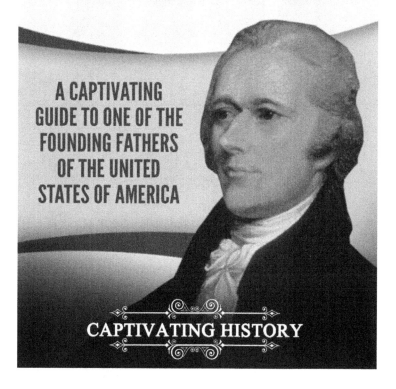

ALEXANDER HAMILTON

A CAPTIVATING GUIDE TO ONE OF THE FOUNDING FATHERS OF THE UNITED STATES OF AMERICA

CAPTIVATING HISTORY

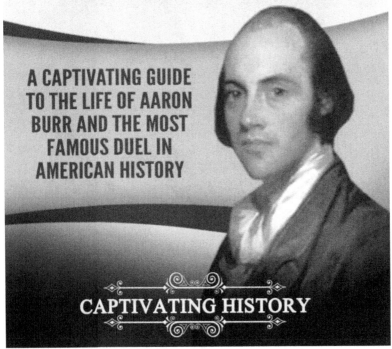

AARON BURR

A CAPTIVATING GUIDE TO THE LIFE OF AARON BURR AND THE MOST FAMOUS DUEL IN AMERICAN HISTORY

CAPTIVATING HISTORY

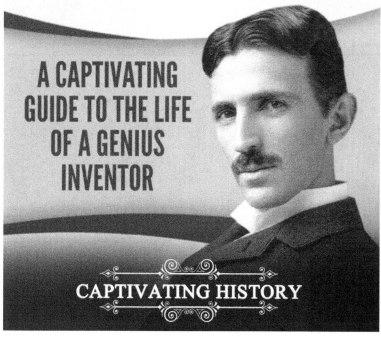

THOMAS EDISON

A CAPTIVATING GUIDE TO THE LIFE OF A GENIUS INVENTOR

CAPTIVATING HISTORY

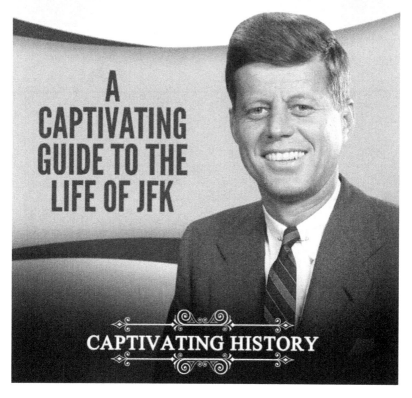

JOHN F. KENNEDY
A CAPTIVATING GUIDE TO THE LIFE OF JFK

CAPTIVATING HISTORY

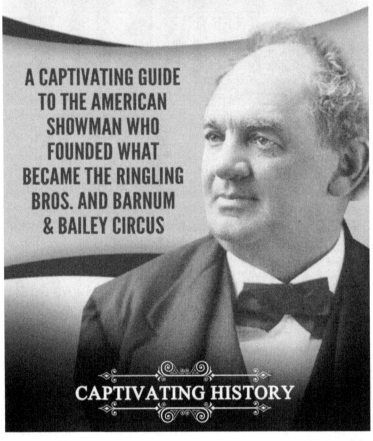

P.T. BARNUM

A CAPTIVATING GUIDE TO THE AMERICAN SHOWMAN WHO FOUNDED WHAT BECAME THE RINGLING BROS. AND BARNUM & BAILEY CIRCUS

CAPTIVATING HISTORY

Sources

Richardson, James D. *A Compilation of the Messages and Papers of the Presidents / Volume 2: 1817-1833*. New York: Bureau of National Literature, 1897.

History, Hourly. *James Monroe: A Life From Beginning to End*. March 21, 2017.

https://www.whitehouse.gov/about-the-white-house/presidents/james-monroe/

http://www.ushistory.org/valleyforge/served/monroe.html

https://millercenter.org/president/monroe

https://www.britannica.com/biography/James-Monroe

https://www.biography.com/news/james-monroe-biography-facts

https://www.biography.com/people/james-monroe-9412098

http://bioguide.congress.gov/scripts/biodisplay.pl?index=m000858

http://www.potus.com/jmonroe.html

http://jamesmonroe.org/

https://www.loc.gov/collections/james-monroe-papers/about-this-collection/

http://academics.umw.edu/jamesmonroepapers/biography/

https://ead.lib.virginia.edu/vivaxtf/view?docId=lva/vi00868.xml

https://owlcation.com/humanities/James-Monroe-Biography-Fifth-President-of-the-United-States

https://www.revolvy.com/main/index.php?s=James+Monroe+Smith

https://history.state.gov/departmenthistory/people/monroe-james

http://www.sparknotes.com/biography/monroe/section5/

http://jamesmonroemuseum.umw.edu

http://highland.org/

https://hsp.org/calendar/spirit-people-james-monroes-1817-tour-northern-states

https://www.arcgis.com/home/item.html?id=5d91f9dadc3f4ff9ad2710d44af68824

https://catalog.hathitrust.org/Record/008650564

https://archive.org/details/tourofjamesmonro00wald

https://www.whitehousehistory.org/articles-of-the-best-kind

https://www.encyclopediavirginia.org

http://www.presidency.ucsb.edu/ws/index.php?pid=25808

https://www.loc.gov/rr/program/bib/inaugurations/monroe/index.html

https://www.cbsnews.com/htdocs/politics/inauguration/history.pdf

https://www.c-span.org/video/?425252-8/james-monroes-life-legacy

https://www.weather.gov/lwx/events_Inauguration

http://www.stateoftheunionhistory.com/2015/07/1819-james-monroe-purchase-of-florida.html

https://history.state.gov/departmenthistory/people/monroe-james

http://www.firstladies.org/biographies/firstladies.aspx?biography=5

http://firstladies.c-span.org/FirstLady/6/Elizabeth-Monroe.aspx

https://www.whitehousehistory.org/bios/elizabeth-monroe

http://www.womenhistoryblog.com/2011/03/elizabeth-kortright-monroe.html

http://www.presidential-power.org/us-first-ladies/elizabeth-monroe.htm

http://fortmonroe.org/lafayettes-visit-to-fort-monroe-in-1824-as-guest-of-the-nation/

http://rmc.library.cornell.edu/lafayette/exhibition/english/tour/

https://archive.org/details/lafayetteinamer01godmgoog

http://flathatnews.com/2015/05/02/making-monroe/

http://academics.umw.edu/jamesmonroepapers/

https://unclesamsnewyork.wordpress.com/2010/02/08/exhuming-president-james-monroe-1758-1831-5th-president-of-the-united-states-removed-from-nycs-marble-cemetery-in-1858/

https://www.varsitytutors.com/earlyamerica/world-early-america/famous-obits/obituary-james-monroe

http://bioguide.congress.gov/scripts/biodisplay.pl?index=m000858

https://www.thefamouspeople.com/profiles/james-monroe-1744.php

https://www.loc.gov/rr/program/bib/ourdocs/monroe.html

https://catalog.archives.gov/id/306420

https://www.ourdocuments.gov/doc.php?flash=false&doc=23

http://www.ushistory.org/documents/monroe.htm

http://www.blackpast.org/gah/monrovia-liberia-1821

http://www.stateoftheunionhistory.com/2015/07/1819-james-monroe-purchase-of-florida.html

https://www.ploddingthroughthepresidents.com/2016/04/james-monroe-famous-paintings.html

https://www.culturaltourismdc.org/portal/war-of-1812

https://study.com/academy/lesson/james-monroes-early-life-childhood.html

http://www.history.org/almanack/people/bios/biojmonroe.cfm

http://www.presidentprofiles.com/Washington-Johnson/James-Monroe-Final-years.html

Made in the USA
Monee, IL
25 October 2020